Dig for Gold

and

Go Rocket!

'Dig for Gold' and 'Go Rocket!'
An original concept by Alison Donald
© Alison Donald

Illustrated by Jo Byatt

Published by MAVERICK ARTS PUBLISHING LTD
Studio 11, City Business Centre, 6 Brighton Road,
Horsham, West Sussex, RH13 5BB
© Maverick Arts Publishing Limited August 2019
+44 (0)1403 256941

A CIP catalogue record for this book is available at the British Library.

ISBN 978-1-84886-610-2

www.maverickbooks.co.uk

This book is rated as: Pink Band (Guided Reading)
This story is decodable at Letters and Sounds Phase 2.

Dig for Gold

and

Go Rocket!

By Alison Donald

Illustrated by
Jo Byatt

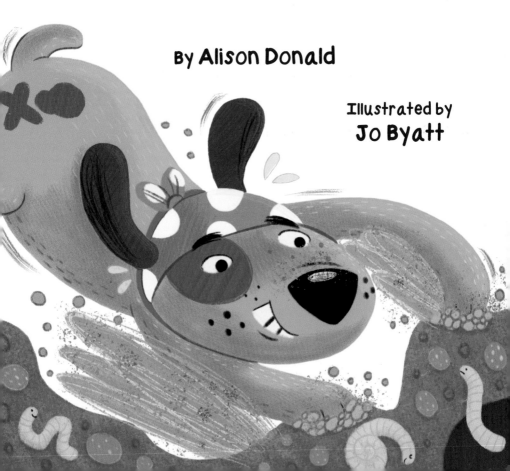

The Letter D

Trace the lower and upper case letter with a finger. Sound out the letter.

Around,
up,
down

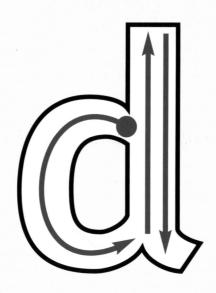

Down,
up,
around

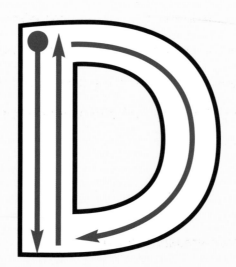

Some words to familiarise:

dig   gold   bone

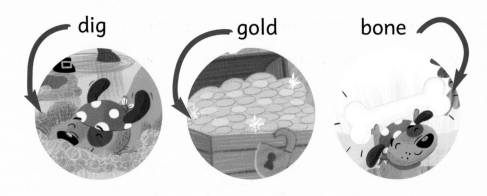

High-frequency words:

a   has   I   to

Tips for Reading 'Dig for Gold'

- Practise the words listed above before reading the story.

- If the reader struggles with any of the other words, ask them
to look for sounds they know in the word. Encourage them to
sound out the words and help them read the words if necessary.

- After reading the story, ask the reader what Dog digs up at the
end of the story.

Fun Activity

Create your own treasure hunt!

Dig for Gold

Pat has a dog.

7

Pat has a map.

9

Pat has a plan.

I love to dig for gold!

Dog has a plan.

Dog has...

...a bone!

The Letter B

Trace the lower and upper case letter with a finger. Sound out the letter.

Down,
up,
around

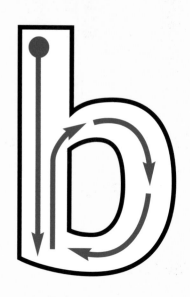

Down,
up,
around,
around

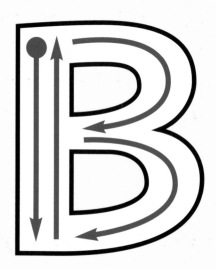

Some words to familiarise:

lab   Bob   shop

High-frequency words:

is   at   the   go   up

Tips for Reading 'Go Rocket!'

- Practise the words listed above before reading the story.

- If the reader struggles with any of the other words, ask them to look for sounds they know in the word. Encourage them to sound out the words and help them read the words if necessary.

- After reading the story, ask the reader where Bob went at the end.

Fun Activity

What other places could Bob have gone to with his rocket?

Go Rocket!

Bob is at the lab.

Bob is at the farm.

23

Bob is at the shop.

Bob is at the park.

Go, Bob, go!

Up, up, up.

Bob is at the moon!

Book Bands for Guided Reading

The Institute of Education book banding system is a scale of colours that reflects the various levels of reading difficulty. The bands are assigned by taking into account the content, the language style, the layout and phonics. Word, phrase and sentence level work is also taken into consideration.

Maverick Early Readers are a bright, attractive range of books covering the pink to white bands. All of these books have been book banded for guided reading to the industry standard and edited by a leading educational consultant.

To view the whole Maverick Readers scheme, visit our website at
www.maverickearlyreaders.com

Or scan the QR code above to view our scheme instantly!